The
84th Infantry Division
in the Battle
of the Ardennes

Theodore Draper
Sergeant, U.S. Army

Merriam Press
Bennington, Vermont
2008

Originally privately published in 1945.
First reprinted by the Merriam Press in 1988.

Fourth Edition (2008)

Book design Copyright © 2008 by the Merriam Press
Additional material copyright of named contributors.

The views expressed are solely those of the author.

ISBN 978-1-4357-5737-0 (paperback) #MM43-P

Printed in the United States of America.

This work was designed, produced, and published in
the United States of America by the

Merriam Press
Bennington VT 05201

E-mail: ray@merriam-press.com
Web site: merriam-press.com

Both the author and the Publisher welcome and encourage
comments and corrections to the material appearing in this work.
Please send them to the Publisher at the above address.

The Merriam Press is always interested in publishing new manuscripts on military history, as
well as reprinting previous works, such as reports, documents,
manuals, articles and other material on military history topics.

For a copy of the current edition of the Merriam Press catalog
describing dozens more Monographs, Memoirs, and Journals
send $1.00 (U.S. first class or foreign airmail delivery).

To order additional copies of this book
visit the Merriam Press web site or write to the address above.

Foreword

AS an ideal, we have always believed that every man should know before every battle what he is going into and why. We have also believed that every man should know after every battle what he, his organization and his army have accomplished and why. In this division, we are trying to live up to that ideal in reports to our men such as this.

Often the after battle orientation is neglected. One action follows another and the last one monopolizes our interest. We miss golden opportunities to benefit from the lessons of experience and to draw inspiration from our accomplishments. In this division, we do not wish to miss those opportunities.

The man in the line who carries the brunt of all the fighting and who deserves all the credit cannot be expected to get the big picture. He has his hands full with the little ones. Primarily this report is meant for him. I think he will find that he will fight better if he knows from past experience that his share was indispensable in the battle, the campaign and the war as a whole.

But I am sure they will not be the only ones to find it interesting and important. The battle of the Ardennes was historic. No history of this war could afford to leave it out. We did something to make that history and now we feel we ought to do something to preserve it. As someone once said, history is the last thing we think about during a war and the first thing we think about after it is over. But then it may be too late.

I hope this will be only the first of a series of such reports. I know that in the years to come, I, for one, will want to read the words, look at the photographs and study the maps. It will bring back memories of days when all of us were tried by fire and came through.

—A. R. Bolling
Major General, U.S. Army Commanding

Contents

Historical Notes

WE have tried to make this report as accurate as possible by using all available records, by personal interviews with key men in as many regiments and battalions and companies as we could reach, by checking and rechecking. We know that many readers will possess far more information about particular aspects of the action than we do. For this reason we would sincerely welcome all suggestions, criticisms, additions, corrections and comments of whatsoever nature. We hope to go over this same ground in greater detail in a future history of the division and we will be able to incorporate new material.

The historical section can only be as good as the material it gets in records, reports and interviews. We hope that this work will show that no time is wasted in giving us full cooperation. For the splendid cooperation that we have already received, we are deeply grateful.

—Lt. Robert E. McHaffie, Historical Officer

At All Cost

EVERY big battle is made up of little battles but it is not always clear what relation the little ones had to the big one. Sometimes the big battle seems to have a life of its own and the little ones do not add up. You have to stand off from the parts and try to see them as a whole before they make sense and fall into a distinct pattern. Much of the fighting in the North African desert was like that.

But there are times when you cannot know what the battle was really like until you get down to the battalions, the companies or even platoons. The little battle is like a perfectly clear pool in which you can see the "big picture" at the bottom. Above all, there is one immense advantage in paying the closest attention to the little picture. Everything becomes more concrete, more realistic. It is not so easy to make vague and sweeping generalities.

What is little and what is big in a battle depends, of course, on where you happen to be looking from. In the battle of the Ardennes, in which many divisions were involved, the story of a single division was relatively "little." No division can claim to tell the whole story or even a major part of it. But there were several divisions which played a role that was like a red thread through the entire action. The 84th Infantry Division was one of them.

In general, the battle of the Ardennes passed through three major phases. The German offensive broke out on December 16, 1944 and lasted in full force for twelve days. The 84th did not get into the beginning of this phase but it more than made up for it at the end. As soon as the German drive was brought to a halt, both sides began to regroup their forces. The third phase, the Allied counteroffensive to wipe out the German "bulge," started January 3, 1945 and achieved its aim on January 16. In this phase, the 84th's part was central.

n the case of the 84th, then, we are able to follow every phase of the battle in the story of a single division. Inevitably, as the fighting went on, the ghost of the French defeat in 1940 seemed to hover over the battlefield.

May 1940-December 1944

BASICALLY, the German breakthroughs of May 10-13, 1940, and December 16-28, 1944, seem very similar. Both General Gamelin and General Bradley took a 'calculated risk' when they decided to concentrate their main forces north of the Ardennes and hold the Ardennes itself with relatively light forces. General von Rundstedt of 1940 and Marshal von Rundstedt of 1944 both decided to strike at precisely the weak point of the Allied line in order to turn the strong point. General von Rundstedt succeeded and Marshal von Rundstedt—we can afford to give the devil his due—made a good try, considering the desperation of his case to begin with.

In 1940, Rundstedt reached the Meuse between Sedan and Dinant, then turned northwest along the Somme River to Abbeville, and boxed in the main Allied forces in Belgium. In 1944, Rundstedt probably tried to reach the Meuse between Namur and Liege, then turn northwest along the Albert Canal to Antwerp, and box in the main Allied forces in Holland and Germany. Not that this was necessarily Rundstedt's expectation; it was probably his fondest hope. But it was perhaps not beyond the realm of possibility and if it had succeeded or had come anywhere near success, it would have been a colossal ease of lightning striking twice in the same place.

In 1940, the German attempt was more interesting than the Allied reaction. In 1944, the Allied reaction was more interesting than the German attempt. In 1940, the French had no forces at all in the Ardennes; they merely tried to rush some in. The Belgians had two divisions of their crack troops, *Chasseurs Ardennais*, and threw them in. The *Chasseurs* were supposed to carry out delaying actions, but delaying was interpreted in a special sense. For the most part, it merely meant demolitions and some half-hearted road blocks. When the Allied command of 1940 thought of the Ardennes, they thought of it as an outpost of the Meuse. The real defense line was the Meuse; the Ardennes was useful only to the extent that some token resistance in the hills and woods would enable the Allied forces to get in position behind the Meuse.

This was the decisive error of 1940 which was not repeated in 1944. For the Ardennes is almost ideal country to defend in. If a strategy of delaying action was at all necessary in 1940, there was no region in western Europe where the enemy could have been forced to pay a higher price for every yard forward. The entire sector is full of commanding high ground. If the hills and ridge lines are held tenaciously, they must be taken one at a time. They can be taken even if they are held quite stubbornly, as our counteroffensive in January 1945 showed, but each attack must come in force and it must be carefully worked out. There is no easy way of racing through. The Ardennes is essentially a forest, from Rochefort south large patches of forest, above Rochefort one small patch of woods after another, often in clusters. These woods provide almost perfect opportunities for pockets of resistance. They can be cleaned out but they must take time and effort. Finally, the region is full of little villages and tiny bits of villages, strategically placed astride the roads. There is probably none which is impregnable but there is none which can be taken without a fight and there are several which might defy any attack for a long time.

There is a popular impression that the chief trouble in the Ardennes is the lack of good roads. As anyone on the ground will agree, the Ardennes has a fairly good road system. It is not the lack of roads as much as the lack of almost anything else on which to move that matters. The extremely woody, extremely hilly country makes it necessary very largely to stick to the roads in the best weather, but there are plenty of roads to stick to. This is where the hills, woods and tiny villages make themselves felt. If they are defended strenuously, advance along the roads may be difficult and costly. On the other hand, if no advantage of these strong points is taken, it may be possible to advance quite rapidly along the existing road net. It should be remembered, too, that the Germans advanced in 1940 in the best time of year, in the middle of May. But even we were able to stage our counteroffensive in the ice and snow of January 1945 when it was even more necessary to stick to the roads at least for our vehicles.

In December 1944, the Allied command faced essentially the same problem as the French did in May 1940. Should we defend in full strength east of the Meuse in the Ardennes or pull back behind the river? The decision of December 1944 was the former. The decision of May 1940 was the latter. Life has already passed judgement on the two but, to get the full value of the lesson, it is necessary to ask why.

At Malmédy, St. Vith and Bastogne, to name only three of the outstanding places, our defense was magnificent and masterful. But some of the other stories may perhaps serve as an even more striking example of the strategic problem as we faced it. We had divisions in or near Malmédy, St. Vith and Bastogne when the Germans struck. But there was one place which at one time was almost wide open. There may be special significance in what we did there.

From Germany to the Ardennes

THREE days after it was launched, the German drive began to ooze southward as its center of gravity, the Malmédy-Stavelot sector, was stopped up. Once blocked at the northern end of the "breakthrough" front, the Germans began to look for weaker spots and for a while they thought they had found one further south in the Ardennes. By December 19, 1944, strong enemy forces were penetrating between Houffalize and Bastogne, a drive which would have led them to the Meuse between Givet and Namur, instead of between Namur and Liege.

In this sector, the principal road centers were St. Vith, Bastogne, La Roche and Marche. By December 22, La Roche and St. Vith were captured and Bastogne was encircled. Unless Marche was held, it was very likely that the Germans would have rolled on to the Meuse.

The Germans were confident that Marche was helpless. The famous demand for surrender which the Germans dropped on Bastogne on December 22 started:

The fortune of war is changing. This time the U.S.A. forces in and near Bastogne have been encircled by strong German armored units. More German armored units have crossed the river Our near Ourtheville, have taken Marche and reached St. Hubert by passing through Homores-Sibret-Tillet.

But the Germans were not the only ones. In Paris, Marche was apparently considered so untenable that, on January 10, twenty-one days after our 84th Infantry Division went in and held it, it was still believed in German hands. What actually happened, however, should help to explain how and why the German drive was stopped dead before it reached the Meuse.

The German offensive opened on December 16. As late as December 18, the 84th was still fighting up in Germany, northeast of Geilenkirchen. In fact, on the 18th, it captured the villages of Wurm and Mullendorf, two strongpoints of the Siegfried Line. It was attached to the Ninth Army whereas the German drive was aimed at the First Army. Yet by the 19th, the 84th was preparing to move about seventy-five miles to the south and by ten o'clock the next evening, December 20, one of its regiments, the 334th Infantry, was already entering Marche. By the 21st, the entire division was safely settled in and around Marche.

In May 1940, General Corap's IX Army had at least three days to move into position along the Meuse between Sedan and Namur, using first-class roads and a railroad, but a large part of his army never arrived in time—Premier Reynaud claimed that as much as half was late. The speed with which some of our divisions were shifted from one front to another and from one army to another in December 1944 was the real counter-surprise to the German command.

The Wide, Open Spaces

WHEN the 84th pulled into Marche on December 20-21, it found itself in virtually a vacuum. The only organized force in the vicinity was the 51st Engineer (C) Battalion which was trying to hold road blocks between La Roche and Hotton and between Champlon and Marche. The "fog of war" was intense. We did not know what to expect in Marche, where the enemy was, how strong he was, or where and how strong our friendly forces were. It was completely unfamiliar ground, the terrain as unlike the country west of the Roer as possible.

It took some time for the fog to dissolve. When it did, we found ourselves right in the path of the 2nd SS Panzer Division and the 116th Panzer Division with nothing on our left flank, above Hotton, and nothing on our right flank, below Marche. For at least three days, the 84th was "out in the breeze" around Marche, an island of resistance to hold back what was momentarily threatening to become a tidal wave of German panzers. It was not until December 24 that the 2nd Armored Division was able to move down between Marche and the Meuse as far as Humain and Buissonville and the 3rd Armored Division was able to connect up with the 84th at Hampteau on the Ourthe.

The big problem those first days was information. If ever a front was "fluid," it was there. The confusion was immense. With no friendly troops on our flanks, it was impossible to get neighboring reports on the enemy's movements. In May 1940, Allied units in similar circumstances almost invariably preferred to pull back to "straighten out the line," to fill in the flanks or to get behind another river. Instead, this time the 84th was ordered to hold the line

Marche-Hotton at all cost. For a single division, this was a huge order. By December 22, our lines extended generally along the line Hampteau-Menil-Verdenne-Hollogne-Waha-Hassonville-Hogne—a distance of no less than twelve miles. Our foxholes were 150 yards apart. And we still had to find out what we were up against.

The position around Marche was uncertain enough but we could cut through the confusion only by plunging even further into the uncertainty. On December 22, two battalions—the 3rd Battalion, 335th Infantry, and the 1st Battalion, 333rd Infantry, were sent out far beyond Marche to organize a counter-reconnaissance screen.

The 3rd Battalion, 335th Infantry, went as far as Tellin, about eleven miles southwest of Marche. The 1st Battalion, 333rd Infantry, went as far as Wanlin, about fourteen miles west of Marche. If we came in without information, we were going out to get some. If we had nothing on our flanks, we were going to send something out. We were going to try to block the roads to Rochefort and Marche ourselves at least in order to buy precious time.

How to Look for Trouble

I F the division was out on a limb, those two battalions went out on the branches. The reconnaissance areas were so large that each battalion had to split up into companies which operated more or less independently and at least one company had to split up into more or less independent platoons.

As for the 3rd Battalion, 335th Infantry, Company I managed to get to Rochefort on the afternoon of December 22. Company L was supposed to go to Hargimont but it ran into heavy resistance at Marloie and could not move any further. The rest of the battalion went to Rochefort by way of Hogne, Sinsin and Haversin to look the ground over to the north and west. At Rochefort, Company K was sent to establish road blocks at Grupont and Tellin, two small villages astride the approaches to Rochefort. Two platoons were dropped off in Tellin and two platoons tried to get to Grupont.

This battalion was now excellently placed to find out where the Germans were. They were all around. By December 23, Company L at Marloie was cut off by enemy forces between Marloie and Rochefort. Late that afternoon, German tanks and infantry started to come into Rochefort. The 2nd Armored Division was coming down towards Rochefort but, for a day, the 3rd Battalion, 335th Infantry, was all we had in the way of the 2nd SS Panzer Division which was racing to a collision with our 2nd Armored.

Company K was out on the leaves of the furthest branch. As the 1st and 2nd platoons were moving from Tellin to Grupont, just as they passed the village of Bure in between, the leading jeep was fired on. A civilian volunteered the information that there were nine Germans and a half-track in Grupont. The 1st platoon went off to Grupont. A German tank rumbled into Bure from Grupont and fired point-blank at the temporary command post. At one point, the company commander, Lt. Leonard R. Carpenter, found himself entirely alone in a house in Bure. When three SS men came in to search the premises, he dove into a potato bin in the cellar, grimly holding on to a 300 radio. After the SS men left empty-handed, he worked on the radio and broke into a conversation which hinted that his two platoons were still in Tellin. With the help of a Belgian civilian—civilians practically saved the company—he found a backwoods trail to Tellin.

At eight-thirty that night, December 23, Company K was ordered to return to Rochefort. There was no way of relaying the information to the 1st platoon which had gone off to Grupont. The rest tumbled into 2½ ton trucks and started back. Outside Rochefort, they found it healthier to proceed on foot. The town was receiving a terrific shelling. In Rochefort, the action was pell-mell. The enemy had infiltrated in force and held most of the houses. Company K moved into a large hotel with Company I. Throughout the night, German 88s, machine guns and burp guns whistled and rattled all over town. We had two 57-mm anti-tank guns and two heavy machine guns in front of the hotel. The next morning, December 24, a German tank came down the street and fired point-blank at the hotel, knocking out several jeeps. A tree-burst of 88s landed in the middle of the crews of the anti-tank guns. By nine-thirty, the battalion was ordered to leave Rochefort but only Company M and battalion headquarters were able to entruck.

Our men in the hotel decided to make a break for it. To cover their movement, they hurled smoke grenades into the middle of the street, blinding a German tank which was waiting for them. They started out the door in a dead run and headed for the railroad tracks to the north of Rochefort. A thousand yards down the tracks, they came to a wooded area. There Lt. Carpenter found he had two-thirds of Company K, half of Company I and a few men from every unit that had ever been in the vicinity.

Company M and battalion headquarters reached Givet at one o'clock in the morning, December 25. From Givet, the trucks went back and luckily found Lt. Carpenter's men on the road. The remainder of Company I ran into elements of the 2nd Armored Division north of Jemelle and came back directly to Marche. Company K's 1st platoon stumbled across some engineers at Chanty who brought them in trucks to Givet. Company L was relieved at Marloie the same day. Those who made the trip from Givet to Marche were constantly receiving reports that Marche had been taken by the enemy. As a result, they went as far north as St. Trond in a big circle. They traveled about 125 miles in thirty-six hours instead of one-fifth the time and distance by a direct route. The whole battalion was back in Marche by noon, December 26.

The efforts of the 1st Battalion, 333rd Infantry, were somewhat similar. On the morning of December 23, Company B was put out in Wellin, Company C in Beauraing and Company A remained in Wanlin. These towns were held until 11 o'clock that night when the battalion received orders to come back. When it received word that the Germans had taken Ciney, midway between Marche and Dinant, it too had to make an enormous circle to get back, going as far north as Namur and Ohey. If the entire column had not turned around in place on a narrow road, it would have twice run into the 2nd SS Panzer which was coming through in force and had tangled with our 2nd Armored.

What did we accomplish? These efforts to block the enemy south of Marche served to delay his advance from Rochefort to the Meuse and to give valuable information of the enemy's strength in this sector and the direction of his thrusts. It may also have served to deflect the enemy's pressure from Marche itself until we were ready to meet it and to give the 2nd Armored Division, which was coming down below Marche, time to get set.

But perhaps the most interesting thing about this action was the attitude behind it. It was conceivable that the division might have decided to sit tight around Marche, waiting for the Germans to come up. Apparently, by December 22, the enemy decided that Marche itself was too strongly held and preferred to go around Marche to the south. The Germans did get as far as 4 miles or so from Dinant and the possible threat of encirclement of Marche was temporarily acute. But, from almost the first moment, the whole conception of holding the Marche-Hotton area was aggressive. Our battalion didn't hold Rochefort but it did prevent the Germans from getting the idea that there was nothing in their way as early as December 22.

The Battle of Verdenne

BY December 24, the fog had lifted for both sides. The 84th was dug in in front of and at both ends of the Marche-Hotton road. Its flanks had been filled in, the 2nd Armored on the right, the 3rd Armored on the left. The 2nd Panzer had twisted south of Marche, penetrating between Rochefort and Hargimont. In a series of great tank battles around Celles, it was badly battered by our 2nd Armored. It was now the turn of the 84th. The 116th Panzer Division, a first-rate outfit, tried to crack the very center of our line. Fortunately, it did not try until we had a line.

In the center of our position was a triangle of villages, Verdenne, Marenne and Bourdon, the latter about a mile in back of the other two. Bourdon was the main objective because it cut the Marche-Hotton road in half. The village which bore the brunt of the enemy's attack, however, was Verdenne because it was the door to Bourdon.

The 3rd Battalion, 334th Infantry, was set up from a crossroads near Champlon to the village of Menu, a distance of about five miles, Company I on the right, Company L on the left, Company K in reserve and Company M in support. On the night of December 23, an enemy force estimated at two reconnaissance companies succeeded in infiltrating behind Company L's position into a woods about a half mile west of Verdenne. The threat was obvious.

At 3 o'clock the next afternoon, December 24, the battle of Verdenne broke out. Strangely, we had chosen that very moment to launch our counterattack on the enemy pocket behind Company K and the enemy had also chosen that moment to attack Verdenne. His plan was to hit Verdenne from the rear with the force in the woods and to hit it frontally at the same time with approximately the same strength. As a result of our counterattack on the woods, however, only half his plan came off.

At 3 o'clock, we sent out Company K, 334th Infantry, and one platoon of Company A, 771st Tank Battalion, followed by Company A, 334th Infantry, to clean out the woods. The Germans had already reached the edge of the woods, intent on their own attack, when our four tanks opened fire on them while our infantry closed in. The German attack was completely broken up and the enemy tried vainly to flee. More than a hundred prisoners were taken in the woods.

But the other half of the German attack, the frontal assault on Verdenne, was temporarily more successful. An enemy force of five Mark V tanks, two half-tracks, an armored car and about a hundred infantrymen drove into Verdenne and continued to move forward as far as a chateau about 200 yards north of the village. That night, the enemy was reinforcing his units in Verdenne and pushed a deep salient into the woods between Verdenne and Bourdon.

Again we had to counterattack. At 1 o'clock the next morning, December 25, Company K, 334th Infantry, and Company L, 333rd Infantry, snapped back. Twenty-five minutes later, Verdenne was ours. It was Christmas morning. All that day, both companies were busy cleaning out the village and chateau, gathering in nine officers and 296 enlisted men as prisoners. The Germans would infiltrate into the village during the night and we had to mop it up for two more days. The total bag of prisoners for Company K alone was 472 before the action was over.

After we retook Verdenne, however, the biggest job was still ahead. When we retook the village, the salient between Verdenne and Bourdon became a pocket of enemy resistance. This pocket was approximately 800 yards long and 300 yards wide in a woods midway between Verdenne and Bourdon. In it were five enemy tanks and an estimated force of two infantry companies. All day, of the 26th, was spent on our part in efforts to eliminate the pocket and on the enemy's part to break through and relieve it.

First we tried. At half past three in the morning, December 26, Companies A and B, 333rd Infantry, attacked the pocket but met strong tank fire and withdrew. Then they tried. At five after seven that same morning, the enemy sent over very heavy artillery fire, followed up by an infantry-tank task force. All our available artillery was immediately concentrated on this attack and broke it up. At eight o'clock, they tried again, this time penetrating our lines approximately 100 yards and four more tanks broke through to join the five already in the pocket. By a quarter to ten, however, our original lines were restored and we turned our full attention to the pocket.

A half hour later, the pocket was hit by units of the 334th Infantry, Company D, 87th Chemical Battalion, and the 84th Division Artillery and four of the nine tanks were knocked out. But the slugging was not over. At a quarter past ten that night, still the 26th, another desperate effort was made to wriggle out of the pocket but the Germans lost three more tanks without anything to show for them. At the end of December 26, our lines in front of Verdenne were stabilized and we had punished the enemy's troops and tanks in the pocket but we were not yet sure that it was completely clear. Only on the following night, December 27, was it possible to send a patrol in to investigate and it reported back that the pocket had vanished. Actually, this enemy pocket between Verdenne and Bourdon, the main threat to our position, was a matter of history by the night of December 26 and our front was quiet by the next night.

There was another flurry on December 26 which helped to discourage the enemy. At about six-thirty in the evening, when two enemy attempts at Verdenne had been repulsed, a strong enemy force, including eight tanks, ten half-tracks, eight motorcycles, a U. S. jeep and about eighty infantrymen tried to break through at another point further north, this time at the village of Menil, between Marenne and Hampteau. As this force came up the road from Marenne, it ran into a "daisy chain" of mines and had to leave the road. The trapped Germans drove right into the positions of Company I and Company M, 333rd Infantry. Bazookas and rifle grenades opened up on the tanks. The enemy infantrymen tried to flee back to their own lines in the woods east of Menil. Three battalions of artillery were fired at the disorganized infantrymen while the vehicles were destroyed in the open field. By seven o'clock, the action was over. Twenty-five enemy vehicles, including six tanks, were knocked out. The failure to break through the Marche-Hotton road was, in effect, Rundstedt's last gasp. The German drive to the Meuse was finished. In the end, Rundstedt had driven some of his best divisions into a big bag in the Ardennes. At the tip of the bag was Marche. A week later, we were going to squeeze it and jam them back.

Post-mortem I

SUCH was the skeleton of the defensive phase of the battle. It can be studied for a long time with profit. Everyone who was in it again learned the old lesson that the way to hold is to hold.

The strategic lesson may be less obvious. The Meuse and the Ardennes are tied together in a single, strategic knot. In 1914 and in 1940, the Meuse was considered the "natural" defense position. No real preparations were made to fight in the Ardennes and, as a result, the Allies were slaughtered in these hills and woods in 1914, or they were not slaughtered in 1940 because they were practically not there. The Ardennes was considered such a formidable natural position that they were counted on to hold up the enemy virtually by themselves. This calculation was tragic both times. By 1940 military engineering had made such advances that it was fatuous.

May 1940 and December 1944 were two sides of the same coin. May 1940 showed that the Meuse could not be held if the Ardennes was not held. This was the fatal mistake which Gamelin and Petain who inspired the whole equipe of 1940 made. December 1944 showed that it was possible to hold the area, that in fact its defensive possibilities were immense. A week later we were going to learn the same lesson when the Germans were on the defensive.

To hold the Ardennes, then, is to hold the Meuse and there may be no other way. At St. Vith, at Bastogne, at Marche, this was demonstrated for the first time. We may be too close to these battles to see them fully but we are perhaps not too close to see what they mean.

The Battle of the Bulge

I F we did nothing else in the Ardennes, we destroyed the myth that the woods and hills of that historically famous battle region are "impenetrable." The Germans began the demonstration in 1940 but their feat was too one-sided to be convincing. They proved it was possible for an army to go through the Ardennes but they did not prove it was possible to *fight* through it. They met real opposition only twice and both times it was a fight of a few hours in clearings within the forest. Above all, the Germans carefully chose the very best time of the year, in May, as if to emphasize that special conditions were necessary. In January 1945, however, we had to fight for practically every hill, wood, village and road, in the very worst time of the year, on ice as slick as grease and in snow waist-high, against skillful and stubborn opposition. The classic, offensive campaign of the Ardennes has been fought and we fought it.

The Big Picture

THE Ardennes campaign may be a hard one to tell about. Every great battle has to be pieced together but in this one the pieces are peculiarly jumbled.

The terrain in the Ardennes is like a jigsaw puzzle. Somehow all of it fits together but somehow all of it can be taken apart and the pieces fall into the oddest shapes. Each hill and wood is like a separate compartment and tactically each one becomes a distinct problem. In this rolling country, there is commanding high ground in almost every mile so that an overnight withdrawal from one hill of defense to the next is relatively easy. The villages and fragments of villages—the toughest "village" to take in our offensive had a single house—are invariably astride the roads and inevitably become enemy strong points. The woods might have been planned by a master strategist to hold pockets of resistance. A continuous offensive or defensive line is impossible. Strong points and pockets of resistance are everything. That is why the battle had such a cut-up, piecemeal character.

The German Bulge was hit from three sides. The third Army came up from the south, from Bastogne. The First Army came down from the north, from both sides of Manhay. The British XXX Corps attacked from the west, from Marche. For us the switch from defensive to offensive was a fine problem in logistics. On January 1, 1945, the 53rd (Welsh) Division began to take over the sector of the 84th Infantry Division while we moved further north. In the First Army's sector, four divisions were involved in the drive—the 84th and 83rd Infantry Divisions and the 2nd and 3rd Armored Divisions. All four had to carry out a complex, eastward side-slipping movement simultaneously on icy, narrow roads, a movement all the more complicated and difficult because two armored divisions were involved. Yet the switch was made amazingly fast. The 84th completed its relief and concentration in its new zone in less than thirty-six hours.

To get the whole story, then, at least three large phases have to be covered—the Third Army, the First Army and the XXX (British) Corps—but the main effort was made by the First Army from the north. The Third Army did not make much progress from the south until the First Army's pressure became irresistible. The 53rd (Welsh) Division was stalled at the most difficult stage of the drive.

In the First Army, the action was conceived as an armor-infantry job—the 84th Infantry Division was teamed with the 2nd Armored, the 83rd with the 3rd Armored. But the main effort was assigned to the 2nd Armored and 84th Infantry Divisions—both La Roche and Houffalize were in their zone of advance.

This offensive from the north was launched between two rivers, the Ourthe and the Salm. By retaking the ground between these two rivers as far as Houffalize, we would hammer a huge wedge through two-thirds of the Bulge. The area between the Ourthe and the Salm was cut almost exactly in half by the road which ran from Manhay to Houffalize (for convenience, it will be called the Houffalize road). This road was the boundary between the 2nd Armored-84th Infantry team and the 3rd Armored-83rd Infantry team, the former on the right near the Ourthe, the latter on the left near the Salm.

We—the 2nd Armored Division and the 84th Infantry Division—were attacking on a front about nine miles wide. The first series of enemy strong points were strung out just below the road from Hotton to Manhay. These strong points—none of them turned out to be very strong—were Trinal – Magoster – Amonines – Lamormenil – Freyneux – Odeigne, less than fifty houses in the largest place. Our ultimate objective was Houffalize, about 16 miles to the southeast. The Third Army, in order to get Houffalize from the bottom of the Bulge, had about half as far to go.

Our zone between the Ourthe River and the Houffalize road was cut in half by a small stream, the Aisne. As a result, at least in the first six days, there were two distinct sectors and the 2nd Armored Division started the attack with two combat commands abreast—Combat Command A extending from the Ourthe to the Aisne, Combat Command B from the Aisne to the Houffalize road. In turn each combat command was made up of three task forces. The set-up was complicated, evidence that the terrain was complicated.

Although our ultimate objective was Houffalize, a midway objective was the road from La Roche to the vital intersection with the Houffalize Road (we will call this other road the La Roche road). The decisive phase of the battle was fought out above the La Roche road in the first week of our attack. By getting to La Roche and especially to the all-important intersection, we would deprive the enemy of the only two good roads which he could use to salvage his force in the Bulge. The mouth of his Bulge would be reduced to the danger point at La Roche to disaster at Houffalize.

As for the 84th Infantry Division, it happened to be placed at the very center of the main effort. One of its regiments drove down to La Roche and another to Houffalize. And there is something else that must be emphasized. Although originally planned as armored offensive, with the infantry in support, the battle of the Ardennes quickly became an infantry attack primarily, with the armor used only as the ground permitted. To that extent, this may be a contribution to the story which is not only typical of the rest but which also traces the line of the main thrust.

The First Day

D-DAY was January 3, 1945. H-hour was 0830. The 2nd Armored Division, to which our 335th Infantry was temporarily attached, attacked to the southeast. The enemy was surprised. Some prisoners were captured asleep. Until noon, we forged ahead steadily. The enemy's outpost line was broken through without much difficulty. The enemy's front was held by three divisions: the 2nd SS Panzer Division on the right near the Ourthe; the 560th Volksgrenadier Division in the center; and the 12th Volksgrenadier Division on the left near the Houffalize Road.

But that morning, in a more important way, our luck ran out. It snowed. Sleet and rain fell in spasms. From early morning the roads were icy. The temperature shot down till the ground was like steel. Tank treads slipped and slid as if the tanks were drunk. Every time a tank skidded, a column was held up. Sometimes the tanks skidded just far enough to block the road.

Trinal was easy. We went in by 0930. By noon, however, resistance was more highly organized and effective. Magoster was harder to crack. After our tanks were held up at several points by enemy bazookas and anti-tank guns, we were able to move in and pass through. The main objective that day was Devantave past a cluster of woods and a hill. The tanks could not get through the woods and our infantry had to push ahead. We got through the woods safely and one company stepped out to cross the hill. Eighty-eights were waiting for them. Eighty-eights and rockets and mortars swept the hill and crashed into the woods. We had to pull back. Light tanks were used to evacuate the wounded; nothing else was possible in the snow. At 1500 hours, we again tried to take

Devantave but again we could not get over the hill. We withdrew for the night east of Magoster.

Farther west that day, it was the same. One company went into Beffe but had to withdraw at night to high ground above the village. Only on the left flank, between the Aisne and the Houffalize Road, was our progress easier. By night, we cleaned out the woods above Odeigne. There was no resistance.

In general, then, the result of the first day's fighting was inconclusive. We had advanced from 1,500 to 2,000 yards, but the enemy's strong points at Beffe and Devantave had frustrated us. It was clear that the enemy was making his main defensive effort on our right flank, between the Ourthe and the Aisne, and his heaviest opposition was reserved for the right sector of the right flank, the hills, woods and villages nearest the Ourthe. This showed that La Roche was the German commander's most sensitive point.

It was still snowing. That was more important than anything else. The roads were bad enough. Icy roads were almost impossible. The hills and woods were formidable obstacles. Knee-deep snow on the hills and woods threatened to give us more trouble than anything the enemy could muster.

Hole in the Crust

FOR four days, we tugged and pulled around Beffe and Devantave. They were the hardest four days the men in this action had ever spent and most of them were veterans of many actions. Then we began to cash in.

The problem of Beffe was typical. It was not so much that the enemy had left strong forces in Beffe itself. It was rather that he was able to pour a deadly fire into Beffe from very favorable positions—from the Consy ridge, about one thousand yards to the southeast, from the Moulin de Bardonive, about one thousand yards to the southwest, and from the direction of Rendeux Bas, a tiny village on the other side of the Ourthe in the 53rd (Welsh) Division British sector. His trump card was direct and observed fire. Although much of the heaviest fighting went on for Beffe itself, the basic problem of this phase of the attack was really the Consy ridge.

The capture of Beffe was also typical. On January 4, 1945, the village was subjected to an intense artillery bombardment. At 1105 hours, Company B, 335th Infantry, began to move in. Meanwhile, Company C, 335th Infantry, retook Magoster and continued on to Beffe. By 1400 hours, both companies made contact at the southern edge of Beffe and dug in. The village was practically deserted.

In effect, after holding us up for a day at Beffe, the enemy was content to give it up, only to fall back to another easily defended position a thousand yards behind. From the first, then, his objective was not so much to hold on to any particular piece of ground at all cost as to delay us and extort the highest possible price for our gains.

The third day, January 5, was another disappointment, our last. At 1 o'clock in the afternoon, the 1st Battalion, 335th Infantry, of Task Force A, launched the main attack from Beffe towards Consy. Company B moved through the woods on the right of the road between Beffe and Consy while Company C moved to firing positions on high ground southeast of Beffe to support Company B's attack. Company A followed behind Company B. After advancing a bit, they received heavy enemy artillery, mortar and machine gun fire from the direction of Rendeux and Rondon on the west bank of the Ourthe. Company B was able to get to the road junction southwest of Consy but met another barrage of the same fire. As a result, the battalion was ordered to return to Beffe for the night. In general, the outcome of the fighting on January 5 amounted to small gains against very strong resistance. On our right flank, the XXX (British) Corps, and on our left flank, the 3rd Armored Division, had the same experience.

When Consy resisted us we turned our main attention to Devantave again. When we took it, Devantave was another deserted village. After our first experience, when we tried to take it from Magoster on the right flank, we organized another attempt, this time from Amonimes on the left. At dawn January 6, 1945, Company I, 335th Infantry, followed by medium tanks, and Company K, 335th Infantry, followed by light tanks, jumped off. By 0930 hours, the tanks had reached the edge of Devantave. At 1100 hours, Company I moved into the western half, Company K the eastern half. Resistance inside the village was light. By 1210 hours, occupation was complete.

With the capture of Magoster, Beffe and Devantave, a deep hole was driven in the crust of the enemy's defensive position on the right flank of our zone. The stage was set for an attack on his most troublesome position, Consy, the "village" with a single house.

Meanwhile, we were still progressing easily on our left flank between the Aisne and the Houffalize Road. The 3rd Battalion, 333rd Infantry, went into action on the second day, January 4, 1945. Company K was sent into Lamormenil, Company L into Freyneux and Company I into the woods west of Lamormenil. All three were taken without difficulty. Tanks went into the village before the infantry. At nightfall, January 5, 1945, Company C and the 1st Platoon of Company D, 333rd Infantry, plus one battalion of a tank battalion, moved out of Le Batty to Odeigne. They met enemy small arms fire but not artillery. The village was completely taken by 1300 hours the next day, January 6, 1945. We did not suffer a single casualty.

Life in the Ardennes

BY the time we took Devantave, it was clear that the original plan which gave the infantry a supporting role was not working out. The terrain and the weather were against it and they won.

The Ardennes is neither roadless nor rich in roads. A British source has estimated that thirteen separate first-class roads cross the Ardennes from Germany to France. There are perhaps three secondary roads for every first-class one and numerous trails. But so many pass through long stretches of woods, so many teeter on the edge of cliffs and wind up and down and around the inescapable hills. In May, too, the possibilities of resistance in the Ardennes would be immense. In January, in snow that keeps piling up from the ankle to the knee, from the knee to the waist, only a little effort is necessary to turn possibilities into realities.

All vehicles have to stick to roads to get anywhere, only more often than not they cannot stick to roads because they are constantly sliding off. The next best thing is to proceed slowly and carefully but then your vehicles may miss the jump-off by hours and the infantry has gone off alone. Is it curious that a terrain that is considered too tough for a tank is never considered too tough for a Doughboy?

If the terrain was bad, the weather was worse. On that morning of our offensive, it began to snow. It snowed all that week. Sometimes the snow dribbled down. At least twice it was as fierce as a blizzard. The official temperature went down to as low as 13 degrees above zero. The trails became invisible. Even in the open, visibility was often limited to thirty or forty yards or less. If ever terrain and weather fought on the side of the enemy, it was in the Ardennes all through our attack.

As a result of the problems which arose in the first four days for the armor, after Devantave was taken, more clearly defined zones for the armor and the infantry began to emerge. From Devantave, the 2nd Armored Division, with the 335th Infantry still attached, veered off more sharply to the southeast to get to Samree through Dochamps, while the 84th Infantry Division assumed responsibility for the drive southward to La Roche and for the La Roche road as far as Samree.

One thing stood out again. When nothing else moved, the Doughboys moved and they moved long and often. And what was it like for them?

In this cold and snow, the problem of taking cover was supreme. It took a good two hours to get through the frozen crust of earth. It took two or three hours more to get down as far as three feet. Not only was digging a foxhole a job in which a whole day's energies could be consumed, but it was practically impossible to dig a really good foxhole at least five feet deep. The weather continued to get colder and colder until it went well below freezing and stayed there. This meant there was only one thing worse than not sleeping—and that was sleeping. The quickest way to freeze is to lie still. Men went to sleep in overcoats—when they had them— and woke up encased in icy boards. It was practically impossible to bring up supplies and rations in anything but half-tracks. Water congealed in canteens. Frostbite was as dangerous as all the Krauts and their guns put together.

The Doughboys who went into Devantave fought ninety-six hours without a break and they were not through by a long shot.

The Turning Point

WE took Consy the way we took most of the strong points—by going around it. When we took Devantave on January 6, 1945, we outflanked Consy on the left. Then we sent two battalions into the woods west of Consy and the enemy was squeezed out in the middle. He did not choose to hold even this commanding position at Consy at all cost. By January 7, 1945, Consy was virtually cleaned out though the woods on the right flank were not completely safe for another two days.

The Aisne River split the 2nd Armored-84th Infantry Division team into two combat teams. Each team drove triple spears at Houffalize to meet the Third Army coming up from Bastogne.

The turning point of the entire action probably came on January 7, 1945, not where we had to fight the hardest but where progress was still relatively easy. On the left flank, after we took Odeigne on January 6, 1945, the 2nd Battalion, 333rd Infantry, was sent out the next day to capture the vital crossroads where the La Roche road and the Houffalize road meet. The weather was miserable. A snowstorm whipped up during the attack. Nevertheless, by 0930 hours, the crossroads were ours. Prisoners, frozen, hungry, and disorganized, were picked up in small, wandering groups. They said they were surprised again. An attack in such harsh weather was completely unexpected. Our interrogators heard that story almost every day.

As soon as we captured the crossroads, the enemy was deprived of the only two first-rate roads to the east, the La Roche road and the Houffalize road. From then on, he must have been inhibited in his intentions, though he would never retire without a fight. Nevertheless, he always had to consider that his chances of successfully pulling his forces out of the trap were getting slimmer and slimmer.

Partly because German resistance above the La Roche road on our right flank was so much stronger than on our left, we were able to cut the road first on the extreme left of our zone at the cross-roads. As we gained full control of the road, we continued to move from left to right. Next, one of our task forces came down from Amonines to Dochamps and from Dochamps we launched the attack on one of the enemy's positions, Samree.

The trip from Amonines to Dochamps was the same old story. The road, though the best in the sector, was so icy and narrow that the tanks were held up repeatedly. Road blocks, which took about two hours each to reduce on the average, some small arms fire but this time very little artillery, represented the enemy's main effort to hold us up. Mine fields and trees felled across the road by detonating TNT charges, anti-tank guns and tanks, were effective sources of enemy resistance. We took the high ground northwest of Dochamps on the night of January 6, 1945, and were able to move into Dochamps the next night. One incident was symbolic. After we had spread out in the village, a German tank with sixty to eighty infantrymen suddenly pulled out from behind the church and made for Samree. Our tank destroyers could not fire a shot because their turrets were frozen, a striking example of weather conditions which lessened the effectiveness of our mechanized equipment and threw the main burden of attack and defense on our infantry.

Samree was seemingly impregnable. It was perched on an 1,800-foot hill. First we had to take two other hills, northeast and northwest of it. Our troops had to move through 1,500 yards of rolling ground in knee-deep snow. The enemy had perfect observation every inch of the way. To tell the truth, it was hard to see how we could make it.

At 0630 hours, January 9, 1945, the 3rd Battalion, 335th Infantry, went out of Dochamps to get those hills. By nightfall, it had progressed to the edge of some woods about 1,500 yards from Samree on the west side of the road and had taken one of the heavily wooded hills guarding the town.

Company L was withdrawn and sent around through Dochamps to occupy the second hill on the east side of the road. That night, our artillery concentrated on Samree. Next day, at 0730 hours, the 3rd Battalion, 335th Infantry, pushed forward to capture the eastern half of Samree and was joined by the 1st Battalion, 335th Infantry, which aimed at the western half. This time, tanks went in first, blazing away their guns, a sight a Doughboy loves best, thinking of all the Doughs it takes to work up that much fire power. By 0925 hours, the village was cleared. We were pleasantly surprised. The enemy was determined to delay us but as long as we showed our determination not to be delayed, we could always take what we wanted.

The infantrymen who went into Samree had been fighting steadily for eight days, for 192 hours. They were certainly helped by the fact that the La Roche road had been cut three days earlier. The artillery concentration on Samree was extremely effective. But in the end, men had to live in some more freezing cold and wade through some snowdrifts, now as much as four and five feet high, to get Samree for us.

The Capture of La Roche

THE battle of La Roche is a good example of the battle of supply and the battle of stamina which every Battle in the Bulge was.

The roads to La Roche were particularly bad, the hills particularly high and the woods particularly dense. A few tanks and trucks turned the snow on the roads into ice and the trouble started. The Doughboys depended more than ever on the Engineers and Artillerymen.

The main attack was launched from Devantave by the 1st Battalion, 334th Infantry. The first objective was Marcouray. Over a hundred guns softened up the village for five minutes. Then, at 1500 hours, January 7, 1945, the infantry jumped off. The ground was rocky and steep. It was snowing again. Thirty minutes later, all German resistance in Marcouray was overrun. We found that the enemy positions were carefully prepared. Snow was a natural camouflage. Fortunately, we were achieving tactical surprises and much of the preparation was wasted. As prisoner after prisoner told us, the weather and terrain were so bad that our infantry was simply not expected. That is one compensation for "impossible" conditions—they are apt to lead the enemy to drop his guard. The enemy's surprise at Marcouray was shown by the equipment he was forced to leave behind. We picked up thirty-six vehicles: eight half-tracks, two command cars, six U.S. jeeps, six civilian type cars, five six-wheeled reconnaissance vehicles, five U.S. tanks, two German ½-ton trucks.

A battle of supplies broke out that night. It was an engineer's nightmare. The engineers dumped sand on the road and put up luminous markers. A convoy of jeeps slipped through with food and ammunition. But two trucks piled into each other, anti-tank guns behind them piled up and the only road forward was blocked. It was blocked all night and part of the next morning. On another road, two prime movers and their guns went over an embankment. Four tanks slid off the road and stuck.

Nevertheless, the attack was pushed. At 1 p.m. the next day, January 8, the doughboys of the 1st Battalion, 334th Infantry, in Marcouray picked themselves up, took what they had and could stuff in their pockets and took off for Cielle, the last little village at the bend of the Ourthe before La Roche. Less than three hours later, they took Cielle the way they had taken Marcouray, only the climb was harder.

Between Cielle and La Roche, dominating the entire bend, was a stretch of very high ground, Hez de Harze, the key to La Roche. Of all our objectives, this was considered the most impossible. An estimated company of enemy infantry was dug in on the forward slope of the hill. The hill was peculiar in one respect. The Germans could see us in Cielle from the hill but it was so heavily wooded that we could not see La Roche from it.

It was the last and hardest part of the job to make La Roche untenable. At 11 a.m., January 9, the 2nd Battalion, 334th Infantry, jumped off from Cielle. Company G led a column of companies to the hill. Enemy tank, machine gun and semi-automatic fire stopped them short. By 12:50, however, Company G had crept up to the base of the hill. Before the advance on foot was resumed, we brought all available artillery and mortar fire to bear on the hill. By 1:10 in the afternoon, as a result of this concentration, the enemy infantry and one tank were seen falling back on the road towards La Roche. Company H's machine guns made the enemy's retreat costly. By 4:10, the 2nd Battalion was firmly established on the Hez de Harze. As it turned out, the chief value of the hill was the fact that the enemy did not have it, but this was no small accomplishment in itself.

The capture of La Roche was relatively uneventful. The first Allied troops to set foot in it was a patrol from the 334th Infantry which entered the town at 4 p.m., January 10. Since half of La Roche was in the 84th Infantry Division's zone and half in the 51st (British) Division's zone, because the Ourthe ran through the town, La Roche was occupied by both divisions. At 9 a.m., January 11, the 4th Cavalry Group, attached to the 84th Infantry Division, took over the eastern half of La Roche which was practically deserted. Two hours later, elements of the 51st (British) Division went into the western half. There was every evidence that the enemy had suffered heavily from our artillery concentrations on the town, once the most beautiful in the Ardennes, and had begun to pull out by January 10.

From Les Tailles to Dinez

WHEN we took La Roche, we sealed the fate of the Bulge. Yet in no sense did it mean that the fighting became less difficult. The terrain and weather were still the enemy's chief allies. His forces had more and more hills and woods to withdraw to. Above all, the German command was now fighting for time, time to regroup and reorganize behind the Siegfried Line, time to meet the overwhelming Russian threat.

There were some significant differences between the two phases. As long as our main objective was La Roche, the enemy's main effort was made on the right flank. As soon as we took the La Roche road and Houffalize became our main objective, the enemy's main effort was made on the left flank. In the second phase, the 333rd Infantry was temporarily attached to the 2nd Armored Division. The 84th Infantry Division was given the right half of the zone, the 2nd Armored Division the left half. In this phase we were faced by elements of the 116th Panzer Division and the 130th Panzer Lehr Division.

As far as the La Roche road, the 333rd Infantry had advanced with relative ease. Once beyond the road, it ran into much more trouble. In Les Tailles and at the edge of the woods to the south, an estimated enemy battalion was dug in. On the other side of the Houffalize road, an estimated reinforced company was holding Petites Tailles. The 2nd Battalion went out from the La Roche road to Les Tailles, the 1st Battalion to Petites Tailles. The experiences of both were significantly similar.

To get to Les Tailles, we had to cross some more woods. The German positions were well camouflaged. The enemy's fields of fire and barrages were well planned to catch us as we came out into the open. At 0800, January 12, 1945, Company F and Company G jumped off. As they came out of the woods north of Les Tailles, they were met by very heavy fire and were held up. At 1500 hours, they began to move again. Ten minutes later, Company G and tanks were entering Les Tailles but the opposition was so sharp that the village was not cleared until 2100 hours. About 140 prisoners were taken.

This happened again and again—we had to fight hard for a place but when we took it we gathered in batches of prisoners. Looked at more closely, however, this phenomenon may tell us a good deal about a German stratagem in fighting this final phase of the war.

Petites Tailles was a striking example. To get to Petites Tailles, the 1st Battalion had to move across relatively open ground down the Houffalize road. The enemy was able to bring direct and observed fire on our troops all the time. A continuous effort was made to approach the village from the flanks but the open terrain made the maneuver difficult. The 1st Battalion jumped off at eight in the morning, January 12, but the enemy's heavy weapons and tanks held it up all day and inflicted heavy casualties. Under cover of darkness, however, we tried again. The fighting was hard but Petites Tailles was ours by nine in the evening. By chance, both Les Tailles and Petites Tailles were cleared at the same time.

In Petites Tailles, we picked up seventy prisoners. Most of them were non-German. The German officers and non-coms had gotten out while the getting out was still good. The rest were left to their own fate without orders. By the time they fell into our hands they were meek indeed. In some instances, they would walk in squad column on the street asking for an "Amerikaner" to surrender to. In at least one case, a group of twenty, completely equipped with rifles and machine guns, tacked on to one of our platoons. In the dark, it is not so easy to surrender successfully.

What had happened? In this village, which cost us so much blood to take, the prisoners were very deceptive. The German officers and non-coms had fled to fight from another village some other day. The prisoners we picked up were the expendables.

Any one of these prisoners behind a machine gun under a tough, experienced German officer or non-com in the middle of the day was one man. That night, in a prisoner cage, he was another man.

From Les Tailles, we had to get to Dinez. To get to Dinez, we had to go through four thousand yards of woods. To go through these woods, we faced problems which were typical of the fighting in the Ardennes forest.

At 0800, January 13, 1945, the 2nd Battalion, 333rd Infantry, jumped off from Les Tailles for the third time in two days. After taking Collas, a little village southwest of Les Tailles, at 1000 hours, it struck out for the woods. Immediately, the terrain became worse than the enemy, though the latter did his best to help. The roads were terrible, barely more than trails. Under the snow, which now had ten days to accumulate, they were invisible. By 1200 hours, the enemy's activity became more stubborn. By the end of the day, we had penetrated only five hundred yards.

The problem of getting through the woods was faced that night. Two narrow trails ran through the woods to Dinez and two special task forces were formed to get through these trails. Both started out at 0800 hours the next day, January 14, 1945.

The woods, snow, cold and narrow trails made supply, evacuation, contact, control and communication a battle of nerves. The only supplies came in with half-tracks. Mortar ammunition had to be carried by hand over two miles. In Odeigne, the 2nd Battalion had captured an enemy horse and sled. They held on to them and in these woods the horse and sled were their only means of evacuating the wounded. Radios would not work in the woods as it was impossible to lay wires. Visibility was so poor that it was always like night in the middle of the day. Since a small group of five or six infantrymen worked with one tank it was hard to put a company or even a platoon together—a troublesome problem for the infantry whenever they work with armor.

Companies F and G rode light tanks part of the way but progress was too slow that way because the tanks were held up so much of the time. By pushing themselves to the limit, both task forces were able to move through the entire woods by 1600 hours. Without stopping once the woods were cleared, Company F attacked Dinez and Company E attacked Willogne. Surprise paid off again. Both were captured before the night was over and about one hundred prisoners were taken in Dinez. Most of our casualties resulted from shell fire and frostbite. We were about 4,500 yards from Houffalize.

One for the Books

MEANWHILE, on the right flank, in the 84th Infantry Division zone, the enemy was wedged in between the La Roche road and the Ourthe River. On the whole, progress was much easier but one minor crisis resulted in perhaps the most unusual experience of the campaign.

The first important objective was Berismenil. At 0730 hours, January 13, 1945, the 1st Battalion, 334th Infantry, moved out from the La Roche road to take a hill about 1,500 yards north of Berismenil. Only sniper fire was encountered and the objective was taken by 1100 hours. At 1415 hours, the 1st Battalion went forward again to take another hill about 750 yards northeast of Berismenil—one of our commanders once said wistfully: "Every time I see a hill, I know it's going to be our next objective."

By 1800 hours, the 1st Battalion had taken its second hill against light resistance. Nevertheless, the situation was confused because orientation in the dark was difficult. When a patrol carrying blankets was fired on from the rear, it was clear that the battalion was almost entirely surrounded by the enemy. Later that night, a reconnaissance patrol was sent to investigate the enemy's position south of the hill but failed to return. Then the battalion commander, Major Roland L. Kolb, decided to see for himself. Leading another patrol, he suddenly observed a German command car pull up to the base of the hill and halt. Two men stepped out and began to walk up the hill. When the pair approached near enough, the patrol jumped out of hiding.

One of their prisoners turned out to be Captain Hanagottfried von Watzdorf, commander of the 1st Battalion, 60th Panzer Grenadiers, 116th Panzer Division. Unaware that his main line of resistance had been penetrated to a depth of more than one thousand yards, the German commander was out on a tour of inspection. In perfect English, he exclaimed: "I am astonished." The commander of one battalion had personally captured the commander of the enemy's battalion opposite him and he had to keep him all night before he could deliver him safely.

Berismenil itself was captured by the 2nd Battalion, 335th Infantry. It covered three thousand yards of trails, thereby achieving a considerable degree of surprise but giving up all possibility of using any vehicles to back up the attack. As a result, Berismenil was captured almost without opposition. By the end of the day, January 13, 1945, the enemy had been cleared out of approximately half the 84th Infantry Division's zone.

The other half was rapidly cleaned out the next day. Nadrin was occupied by the 1st Battalion, 334th Infantry, at 1130 hours, January 14, 1945. Only some machine guns and small arms resistance was encountered. At the same time, the 3rd Battalion, 334th Infantry, attacked Filly, about a mile southeast of Nadrin. Tanks and tank destroyers could not use the roads because they were heavily mined and the infantry went on alone. Filly was entered at 1530 hours without any artillery preparation and fully occupied a half-hour later. The 3rd Battalion went on to take the last two objectives, Petite-Mormont and Grande-Mormont by 1915 hours.

By this time, the Bulge was practically a memory and the chief interest of every commander—company, battalion, regiment, and division—was how to send out the patrol to make the first contact with the Third Army.

End of the Bulge

WE made Houffalize completely untenable on January 15, 1945. At 1100 hours, the 1st Battalion, 333rd Infantry, jumped off from Dinez and captured the village of Mont, midway between Dinez and Houffalize, by 1400 hours. Tanks, infantry, and artillery worked together smoothly. At 1600 hours, the advance was renewed to Hill 430, overlooking Houffalize. It was taken by 1730 hours without opposition.

Credit for going into Houffalize went to the 2nd Armored Division. The 1st Battalion, 333rd Infantry, held Hill 430 until 1700 hours, January 16, 1945, when it was relieved by a reconnaissance element of the 2nd Armored Division. By 1745 hours, January 16, 1945, elements of the 2nd Armored held the northern part of Houffalize, while elements of the 11th Armored Division held the southern portion.

When was the Bulge wiped out? That may never be decided to everyone's satisfaction because a number of patrols were frantically trying to make contact with a number of other patrols at the same time. I can merely report how and when the 84th Infantry Division closed the Bulge for itself.

A thirty-three–man patrol, led by Lieutenant Byron Blankenship, representing the 334th Infantry, left Filly at 1100 hours, January 15, 1945. At 1145 hours they crossed the Ourthe in two 400-pound rubber boats, which they carried. The rest of the afternoon they spent in an old mill on the other side of the Ourthe. Just before dark, Lt. Blankenship led a small patrol into the village of Engreux, about one thousand yards from the Ourthe, where he expected to meet a patrol from the Third Army. He found the village free of the enemy but he also found no sign of the Third Army's patrol.

Late that night, Lt. Blankenship received word that the rendezvous had been changed. Starting off again at midnight, the patrol moved out across some more woods and over a 1,200-yard ridge. At 0220 hours, January 16, 1945, in the dead of night, they stopped at a small Belgian farmhouse. The whole family, papa, mama, a son and a daughter of 22 turned itself into a reception committee. There were bread, butter, and hot coffee. The patrol decided the rendezvous had been changed for a good reason.

That morning at 0930 hours, PFC Rodney Himes, second in command of the patrol, spied a soldier walking outside the farmhouse. Since the patrol had been ordered to stay inside the house, PFC Himes began to "Bawl him out" and asked him "What outfit he was from." The answer was a platoon of Cavalry from the 11th Armored Division, U.S. Third Army.

The junction was officially achieved at 0945 hours, January 16, 1945, by Lt. Blankenship of the 334th Infantry and Lt. Lucas of the Cavalry. The Bulge was wiped out after thirteen days of hard, continuos fighting on the morning of January 16.

Beho to Gouvy to Ourthe

WE rested five days and on the sixth day we went into battle again. This time we moved up north to do our part in the drive to take back the last bit of ground which the Germans had seized in their December offensive. The big objective was St. Vith.

This drive was actually begun on January 13, soon after La Roche fell and the German withdrawal all along the line was well under way. The 30th and 106th Infantry Divisions came down toward St. Vith from the north, from the direction of Stavelot. Two days later, January 15, the 75th Infantry Division attacked from the west, from the direction of the La Roche road, and Salmchateau fell. On January 19, the 30th Infantry Division took Recht and the 1st Infantry Division cleared a defile on the 30th's left flank. The next morning, January 20, the 7th Armored Division launched the final attack at St. Vith, also from the north, but it was held up at Born which did not fall until nightfall of the next day, January 21. From Born to St. Vith were two more miles. As the 7th Armored was preparing to close the last gap, the 84th Infantry Division was preparing to clean out the area to the south midway between Houffalize and St. Vith.

Our objectives were the villages of Beho, Gouvy and Ourthe. As operations go, it was not a major operation. After taking all there was to take in our original zone, we were helping out in the last stage of the action in the zone next to ours. But to the men who fought for those three villages, the battles were every bit as important as any other battles anywhere. They were just as hard, just as bitter. Men died, dug for cover, ducked 88s, bandaged up buddies if they could, the same way. It was still cold. The snow was three to four feet deep. Vehicles still could not get off the roads without staying off permanently. There were many bridges in our new zone and all were down. Tanks, heavy machine guns, artillery and rockets were still at the enemy's disposal. As far as the man in the line is concerned, war is funny that way. There are big objectives which make big headlines that are relatively easy to take. And there are little objectives which nobody notices that had to be bought with blood yard by yard. For the man in the line, the big battle is the little one.

From our lines to Gouvy was a distance of approximately 2,000 yards but approximately 5,000 yards separated us from Beho. On our right flank, the main enemy strong points were the village of Gouvy and the railroad station about 1,000 yards east of the village where the enemy was prepared to throw in tanks, anti-tank guns and infantry. At eight o'clock in the morning, January 22, the 2nd Battalion, 335th Infantry, jumped off towards Gouvy. At first, the advance was slow and difficult because weather conditions were so trying and the enemy was able to take advantage of observation from the front and the high, open ground to the southeast. But continued pressure forced the Germans to withdraw east of the railroad. At 1250 hours, Company G entered Gouvy. In the woods northeast of Gouvy, however, the 2nd Battalion met heavy resistance from dug-in infantry, supported by tanks.

Beho was attacked at the same time from both flanks. The 334th Infantry came down on the right, the 333rd Infantry on the left. Two battalions worked different routes for both regiments. On the right flank, the 2nd Battalion, 334th Infantry, started out near the village of Halconreux to the southwest and had to cross about a mile and a half of thick woods to get to Beho. The 3rd Battalion came down the road from Bovigny to the northwest. On the left flank, the 1st and 2nd Battalions, 333rd Infantry, came down on both sides of the road from Rogery to Beho, a bit further to the northwest, the 1ˢᵗ Battalion on the left side of the road, the 2ⁿᵈ Battalion on the right side.

The chief resistance was encountered by the 2ⁿᵈ Battalion, 334ᵗʰ Infantry. At 6:30 in the morning, January 22, the 2ⁿᵈ Battalion jumped off from the edge of woods west of Halconreux. Company F went through the village twenty minutes later, meeting no opposition. It was planned to get the whole battalion into the woods between Halconreux and Beho before daylight but the snow and hilly ground made this impossible. At about 0730 hours, as the battalion was approaching the railroad at the western edge of the woods, enemy small arms fire, supported by mortars and at least three tanks, opened up. This burst of resistance held up the battalion until 1:30 in the afternoon when a way was found to bypass the opposition and the battalion succeeded in pushing forward into the woods.

Meanwhile, the 3ʳᵈ Battalion, 334ᵗʰ Infantry, was moving down the Bovigny-Beho road. By four o'clock in the afternoon, it had reached a point on the eastern edge of the woods from which to launch the final assault on Beho. In the original plan, the 2ⁿᵈ and 3ʳᵈ Battalions were going to make a coordinated attack on Beho but the snow and dense forest were slowing down the pace of the 2ⁿᵈ Battalion. At five-fifteen, when it seemed clear that the 2ⁿᵈ Battalion might not be able to participate in the joint attack before dark, the 3ʳᵈ Battalion was ordered to take Beho alone.

After a heavy artillery concentration, the 3ʳᵈ Battalion moved into Beho. The village was occupied by eight o'clock that night. At this, the enemy force in Beho tried to withdraw to the north, only to find itself in the direct path of the 1ˢᵗ Battalion, 333ʳᵈ Infantry, which had meanwhile been coming down from Rogery.

At 0815 hours that morning, January 22, the 1ˢᵗ Battalion, 333ʳᵈ Infantry, had jumped off from Rogery and had pushed on to the high ground about 400 yards northeast of Beho by 0530 hours that evening. Two hours later, when the enemy force in Beho tried to withdraw to the northeast under pressure of the 3rd Battalion, 334th Infantry, it ran straight into the 1st Battalion, 333rd Infantry. For more than an hour, the fight raged. Some of the heaviest action of the day took place northeast of Beho as the enemy was driven to the east by our artillery and small arms fire.

Meanwhile, the 7th Armored Division was pushing down to St. Vith to which the enemy was still grimly holding on, the last prize of his Ardennes adventure.

The Last Mile

THE next day was spent securing Gouvy and Beho, our primary objectives, from enemy counterattacks. To secure Gouvy, we had to take the village of Ourthe. At 7:45 in the morning, January 23, the 3rd Battalion, 335th Infantry, moved out along the Gouvy-Ourthe road. As the leading elements of Company K advanced to the edge of Ourthe, the enemy on the high ground to the east and southeast opened up with automatic weapons, heavy mortars and small arms. The advance was halted. Company I was sent to attack Ourthe from the north but came under the same fire. Our artillery was then called on to soften up the enemy force in Ourthe. Under cover of smoke, artillery and mortar barrages, Companies K and I, with the support of Company C, 771st Tank Battalion, started forward again at nightfall. This time, Ourthe was ours.

At Beho, the problem of securing our gains turned out to be the problem of repelling a strong, enemy counterattack. Once more it was demonstrated that the enemy, far from resigning himself to permanent loss of initiative in our zone, would try from time to time to wrest it from us.

At six-thirty in the morning, January 23, the 2nd Battalion, 334th Infantry, renewed the attack from Beho to seize the high ground and crossroads about a thousand yards east of Beho, between Beho and Audrange, and the high ground about two thousand yards southeast of Beho. By seven o'clock, Company E had surprised the enemy outposts at the crossroads and had occupied a nearby monastery. By 0830 hours, Company G had taken the other objective without resistance and had begun to dig in. But the day's fighting for Company E was not over.

At eight-thirty, a force of two hundred men from the 20th Panzergrenadiers, 9th SS Panzer Division, supported by three tanks, approached from the direction of Audrange. The tanks began to shell the monastery. Fortunately, the walls were exceptionally thick and the fire had little effect on our men. At the same time, the German infantry closed in. Backed by tanks, this threat was more dangerous. To meet the critical situation, Company B called for artillery on the monastery itself. When our shells began to land with deadly effect in the very yard of the monastery, the tide began to turn.

Meanwhile, Company F had been sent out to relieve Company B. When Company F arrived on the high ground southeast of the monastery, as many Germans as were still alive beat a hasty retreat to Audrange. By nine o'clock, the crossroads was quiet again. In effect, our share of the battle of the Ardennes was done.

Post-mortem II

WHAT did we accomplish? The Battle of the Bulge was one of the hardest, if not the hardest, fight of the Allied armies in Europe. The weather, the terrain and the enemy combined to make a campaign of peculiar bitterness and difficulty. Many veteran observers considered it worse than anything they had seen.

But it paid off. It was estimated that the German command invested twenty-eight divisions in the Ardennes. By the time we launched our counteroffensive on January 3, the enemy had probably lost about 90,000 men in the vain effort to break through to the Meuse and had about 134,000 left. The enemy's losses in equipment were just as important, if not more so. It was estimated that the Germans moved 40,000-50,000 vehicles of all kinds into the Bulge. In tanks, the 84th Infantry Division alone accounted for forty-seven. The Germans probably lost a greater percentage of vehicles in the Bulge than men. Despite the fact that the enemy fell back to the Siegfried Line without serious disorder on the whole, we did take about a thousand prisoners a day in the last week of the Battle of the Bulge. From these indications, it may be seen that a hard, if not a staggering, blow was struck at the German Army in the west in the five weeks of the fight in the Ardennes.

What may we safely conclude?

The Allied armies in the west, and our own army in particular, showed that panic was absolutely alien to them. An extraordinary situation arose. An extraordinary effort was made to dispose of it. The Germans were just as much surprised, if not more so, by our amazing ability to bounce back as we were surprised by his original blow. The first German prisoners we took were pretty cocky. They thought it was 1940 all over again. A good many really believed the story that the Führer would be in Paris in three weeks. In a week, they were not so confident. In ten days, all hope was gone. The prisoners showed intense depression. We had scored a psychological as well as a material victory. Even the stupidest or the most fanatical now knew that the game was up.

It is interesting to note that the Red Army waited until the German Command had fully committed its last reserves in the Ardennes before the unprecedented offensive in the east was launched. At a time when the common enemy needed every available man and gun and vehicle in the east, we had the reserves in a vise in the west. In this sense, we made as important a contribution to the Russian victory as if we had been fighting in East Prussia, in Poland or in Silesia. In the same way, once the Red Army's tide swept into Germany, the enemy tried frantically to extricate himself in the west. In this way, our Russian allies made as important a contribution to our victory in the Ardennes as if they had been fighting in Devantave, in Samree and in Les Tailles. In this global war, a little pressure in the right place may go a long way.

We have fought other battles and we will fight others but none of those who were in it will ever forget the one in the Ardennes. If we came through, by far the largest credit must go to the men who shouldered rifles and carried machine guns and mortars in freezing weather, plunged through knee-deep and waist-high snow, dug foxholes in ground as hard as steel, stormed hill after hill in the face of perfect, enemy observation and cleaned out woods as dark as night in the middle of the day. That is not the whole story but it is the best part of it.